Pancakes for supper

supper

Liz Lewis

Geographical Association

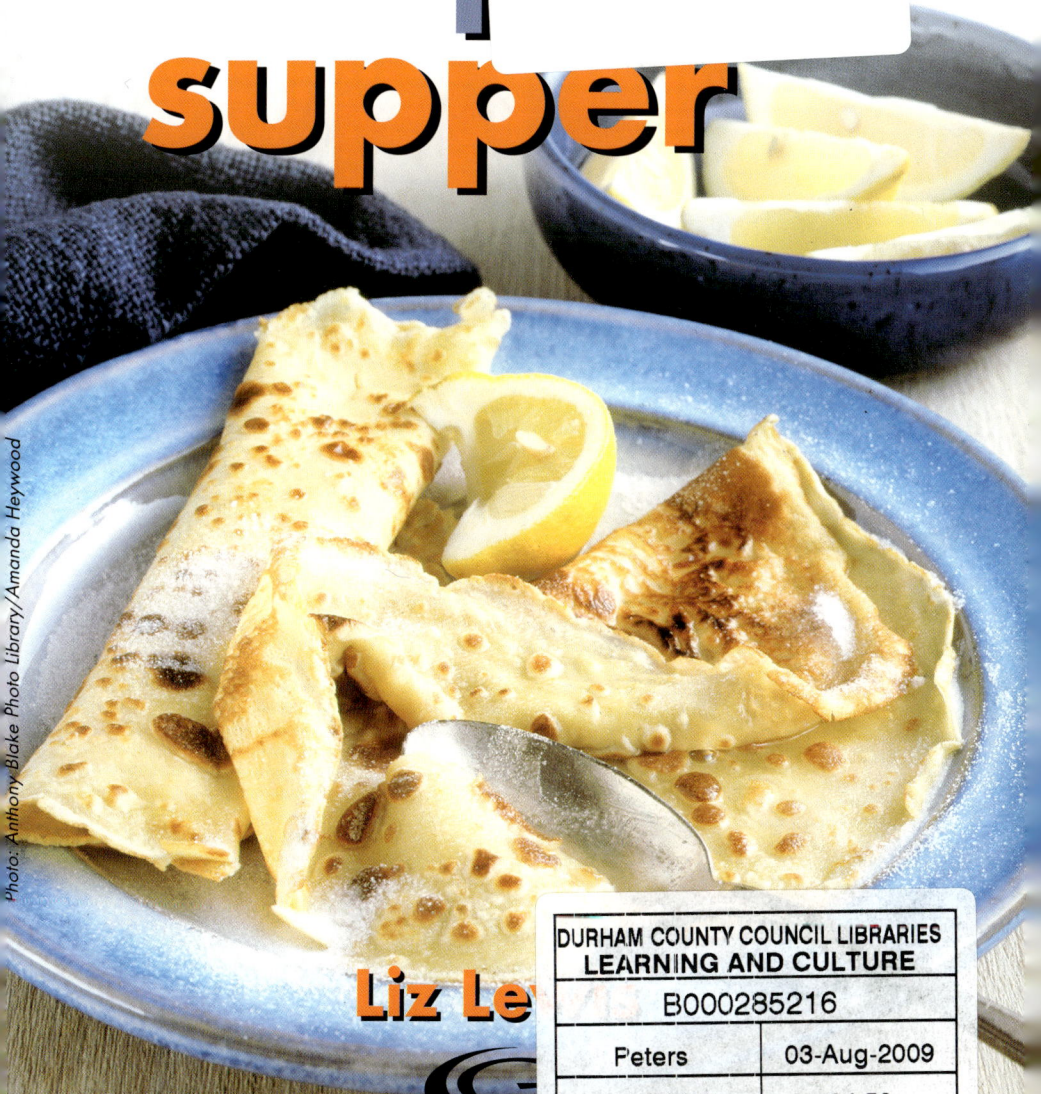

Barnaby goes with Mum and Nan to
have pancakes for supper.
They look at the menu.
Mum tells Barnaby what the French
words mean.

Crêpes

Nan and Mum have pancakes with ham and eggs. Barnaby thinks chocolate and ice cream sounds better!

The bears enjoy their pancakes.
'How do they make them so thin?'
Barnaby asks Mum.

'I don't know, Barnaby. Shall we ask the cook?' says Mum.

Nan tells the cook how much they enjoyed their pancakes.

How do
you make
pancakes,
please?

The cook puts flour in a bowl. She makes a well in the flour. She puts the eggs and milk in. Then she begins to mix it.

'You have to beat until your arms hurt,' she says. 'Here, have a go, Barnaby.' Barnaby beats and beats until his paws hurt. He makes a lovely smooth batter.

The cook has a big flat pan on the cooker. It is very hot. 'Stand back, Barnaby, while I put the batter in the pan,' she says. 'Listen, it will sizzle.'

The pancake is nearly ready. The cook helps Barnaby to toss the pancake.

The cook gives Barnaby extra ice cream and chocolate sauce with his pancake. 'Bon appétit!' says the cook.